Mario

crib

ENITHARMON PRESS

First published in 2014
by Enitharmon Press
10 Bury Place
, London WC1A 2JL

www.enitharmon.co.uk

Distributed in the UK by
Central Books
99 Wallis Road
London E9 5LN

Distributed in the USA and Canada
by Dufour Editions Inc.
PO Box 7, Chester Springs
PA 19425, USA

ISBN 978-1-907587-80-1

British Library Cataloguing-in-Publication Data.
A catalogue record for this book is available
from the British Library.

Typeset in Albertina by Libanus Press
and printed in England by
Antony Rowe Ltd

crib

ACKNOWLEDGEMENTS

I am grateful to the Royal Literary Fund and to the Arts Council England (London) *Grants for the Arts – Individuals (Lottery)* Fund for their support. Thanks are also due to the editors of the following publications and websites where versions of some of these poems first appeared: *Acumen*, *Antiphon* (antiphon.org.uk), *Dark Mountain*, *EarthLines*, *Entanglements* (Two Ravens Press, 2012), *The Interpreter's House*, *Iota*, *KJV: Old Text ~ New Poetry* (Wivenbooks, 2011), *Languages of Colour* (The Frogmore Press, 2012), *London Grip* (londongrip.co.uk), *New Trespass* (exacteditions.com), *Of Love and Hope* (Avalanche Books, 2010), *Poetic Pilgrimages: James Hogg at Eighty* (Poetry Salzburg, 2011), *Poetry & All That Jazz* (focus:arts(chi.uk), 2012), *Poetry and Audience*, *Poetry Express* (survivorspoetry.org), *Poetry Wales*, *Scintilla 16* (The Vaughan Association, 2012), *Wenlock Poetry Festival Anthology* (Ellingham Press, 2011), *Wenlock Poetry Festival Anthology* (Ellingham Press, 2012).

A rework of *it comes to you so* was shortlisted for the Bridport Prize 2011. *what pours* was presented at the British Council *Festival Innovarte* (Madrid: November, 2010) and at the *Reading Nature* conference held at the Universidad Complutense (Madrid: December, 2011).

I thank Adam Simmonds for his helpful comments, and am particularly indebted to Jacqui Rowe and Peter Brennan for having travelled with me through these poems, offering insightful suggestions and profound encouragement at many junctures. Most of all, I wish every blessing upon Annie, for making Mattie possible.

*

As context, I should note that *crib* is a selection of 40 poems – all but the last presented here chronologically – from the total of 111 written for my son towards the end of 2008 through 2009, the 111th poem arriving exactly 1 year after his birth (with his mother aged 39). This series forms a clear sub-sequence within the overall *i tulips* project of 1111 poems. In terms of Enitharmon collections, *crib* provides the second instalment of extracts from that larger enterprise; the first was published in March 2010 under the title *i tulips*.

-

Cover photograph by the author: *Mattie – 1*.

CONTENTS

for Matteo

"words are the daughters of earth . . .
things are the sons of heaven"

Dr. Johnson
(Preface to the Dictionary)

" . . . a child, the produced babe of the vegetation"

Song of Myself 6

monitor i

put palm to
you the day before
head-down lefty

lost
to that book
of yourself

snug in
domed antisocial
amniotica

hanging put
a gallop to keep
worlds waiting

as we heat-seek
the name – infantile
type naught-head

half-set nothing
to argue with
sweet-dark

pumpbubble
heart gorgeous
with sleep

an odd kick
balling your fists
coldwater sugar

post hoc
amorino refusing
through ticker-taped

swell what
we reasonably
desire : on

-going pa
-limpsestic thud
bed & rail

defer to till
nurse peels you
for your album –

digital analogue
down fine-griddled
snowpaper nearing

furthering im-
palpables par-
enting hands

half-stalk

this throat that

comes smeared with
birth-fat yet
widest

hardest
part-first exposing
whelmed through light

-sudden word skin on
redlettery skin –
they

say
feed you straight
ways : take your tonsil-pink

up & in before world
should dampen
down

but i now
made by you to
look not *at* would

deliver whatever blood
-sound   through
pushing

throat-
first the wide
legged mother forgotten

almost to have you sound
-brimming ungrown
who shake

with silence

my hand cups

headbulb
shallowly planted
by blanket fine-haired

cheek versus palm its
tiny short-lived
shocks

of sap little
god in seven days
you have doubled folded

-mother intofather how
first crocus folds
spring from

flushwhite
fuse entering
winter reneging

soiled sleep taking
it new space
bubbled

white in
still dark you
float through un-

attached

cloud & face

again vaporous
each shifting at inner
strata : chemical strategies

that siphon milk to lips
or eyes to dark
under

-rind half-
expecting lightning
to dart earthward bearing

something fresh – though
this latter light eased
& lengthened

from its bolts
grown gentler with
afternoon gives one brief

smile westward : parting
pink nimbus onto
milky

anterior
– for this small
honest breath of the new

boy on the world
chock who
looks

& looks as we
do hoping
to see

one boy

that complex guttural
bathplugs
make

endless
glottal stops
culled from swamp

small bib-talk in
a stomach
never

growing
up – that slow
suck of flesh sweeter

off stone as though
a peach could
kiss

son –
through stone
flesh air each care

-conducting sound how
ever botched or
parched

seems
with or with
out us a world world

bent on speech

splaying out

your jitterbug
stops whenever my
block dry-docks

steady barging skull
homes & that
bodied bay you make

oversmall for looming
swerve of adult
hull embraces the face

in jerk-silk arms your
cheek faintly
averted reddening stills

as Grecian light dwells
in low-lying
sun docketing washed

-out verticals with
each wave that laps
lungs correspond &

quell as sighs in-
still what eyes not
quite meeting

meet : selves
old with being held
in the new &

time blood-
grasped plunges blood
-slow rasp

to sleep

airs i

am suddenly
privy to because
sun swayed into this

room & eyes after
fifty years set
square

to show
that plume my
body makes bowing to

low-slung stratospheric
ceiling or cirrus
puffs her

breath chugs
behind rounding
our bend the fig freshly

open at its ungardened
end sloughing
warmth

upwards
in leaf-sized
slats & this boy

laying off skinned
heat— gos-
samers

that rise
to jelly
fish

ours

before speech-vow

-el swirls
mouth–bound for
incarnation dummied

lips miss it shimmying
simian sound ex-
tending

flesh to
the halfsaid you
say therefore found &

send us in liquids surd
-brown sudded as
wavelets to

shores close
scanned each pebble
you put down rocked in sung

singularity as hundred
-yarded water
world

speaks rears beyond
walls immensely
blackly

nouned

a closed door on

you makes it
fill outwards as
ice swells its pond

sealing odours shoots
sent thinned
straight

down as roots
tend a stone or
winter one   toad

white with cold & me
breathing breath as
though syrupy

locked in
here un
able to

stir

*

      faint
with striations
fine as down yet

elongated tensile as
steel reaching
past &

through
as if a woman
large as any house &

more dark neither
sees stood just
over rafters

as night closed
in & leaning hung
long hair low to

matter to fill your cot
& you with thickly
invisible faint-

stranded light

i watch childbody

locked out vowelled
arms consonant
hands mis-

-jointed as when
language sprouted
from its rock put that

cleft in tongue's soft
bulk & corposant
genes still

frayed cocked
close at brain's dial
aglow for any combination

so you could now
play it out
click

anti click
slide the phonemes
you barely know soon

something cog-deep in
you must (calm
as a dropped

clock)
snick so
sound's sound

-heavy door can
swing & hands
half tried half

milk reach in

i fish

in dark
with dark
as spool &

mark him
sparely
move

as if
i sought
magnified

on glass slide
that form
nekton

slow
-slewed
on current i

use him to
snag but
find me

caught

what pours

from that so-fast
treading there
just under

where rib
might be – your
one tight curd in muscle

throwing itself back &
through & always
back   angry

with life
it fills with or
empties hung in

you as a red wasp
in almost too
small

a web?

when a gaze

is
not yet
thunder but

merely rolled open
steeped in
sleep

still
finding
range &

target that look
before a look
occupies

as if skies
found a way to
blink till then stup-

endously unwatched &
overseen you
lift blue

at last to
me – a glance
through wonder that

once thrown seemingly
fixes all that has
passed

below

when bone breaks

up those twin stelae
skewed offline
by time

twisted
slightly trans-
lucent with moonlight

pushing up & through
that last perfect
ridge

inner body
presents as gum
bones old civilisations

sending up their dead this
enamelled voodoo
over

night
pulsing cheeks
redder bloodier its cave

that yawns to gnaw each
cry from the white-
ribbed cage for

bone
breaks bones
to continue as child

drawn to rest through
it – its voiceless
endless

messenger

it comes to you so

heavily only death
in you could
resist

that darker
transfusion w-
ashed through you

till curdled blood
takes on bluest
hue to burn

in brain its
purpler flame
cool enough for

thumbs to twinge in
– yet every dusk
your torso

finds fresh
positions to perturb
the passed who press

from corners resembling
coalescence of all
the failed &

worn-out
silvering as they
inch in to spin you

shards your slumber
rearranges never
drawing serum

or shattered
reflection – even
tonight with one arm

flung as though guylines
snaked a forearm to
hoist you

signalling
hours : Ahab
returned shaved

of time to fall back
into the blue
sheet

chin-soft &
at peace with
sinking in back

-ward embrace to
his still-white
whale

of sleep

what wakeful work

to jerk out
fists & up to keep
sleep's transparent maw from
closure though now it
clamps you

from below to
slow & billow you
spine to chest dampened sense
half-clung to lashes
as dew

about to con
densate that jet
sun inverting defence so all
struggle continues
darkly inward

till i see eighty
years hence the cot
-bound time-worn baby
reaching one fist out
for mothers

long dead

close in   in

pungent waves you
enter   as i lean
to breathe

you breath
-perfumed your
aromas skimmed kin

-like from that benthic
bulk you are to
molecules

sealing their
salts beneath skinned
light or squirming shoals

corpuscular under salten
burdens your lymph
circulates as

turtle or salmon
cogent in whatever
underwatered bodies must

do you drowse as aware
as the egg that sleeps
inside the egg :

your pink-lit
face reduced &
reflected zeroed

in this eye

you carry it

with you far out
from itself into a half
-sunned hall where once

nonna made to wait drew
it in nodding foreign
& chin-heavy on

the bottom stair
or from high chairs
you sense it pushing in

from behind so swat it
forwards into paste :
beastly twin half

kept upstairs to
snout breath darkly
or slow hearts & homes

to that odd pulse – any
corner of the house
laid bare to it

as lids droop
-drip before you
are carried slumped

into that different skin
flaccid & pointless
healing animal

within never
healed so half-way
dark it brings bright arms

low & reaching

as fruit whelms

your peach-heavy head
its velveteen film
misshapen by

shade croaching the branch
– chin a white pear's
unpecked half

sheared by the fall with twin
-meloned rear flecked
& lids raspberry

-crushed after crying you hush
sap to push out thick-
gummed p-

rune as though elements were
stacked for harvested
child laid out in

summer full on its stalk &
so alone in bedstraw
that sin

-gle wild strawberry
perched on your
neck

night tentative

bestrides you
stripes you less tigercub
than resistor – your quiet ohm

almost tubular in gloom precision
made precariously singular
conducting headcot

to basecot what
flows through long
hours whose odd fizz or

jump bears in from stars full
-charged to interrogate
that whitish sub

-stance compressed
with purpose steadied in
you who signal on these far

-off boards intensest heat's
smallest most vital
dissipation

it comes by

increment : iris
crescents nervy in
their lucid element not

sky nor water but move
-ment that spurs &
engorges

movement
begun as each
lid twitched to near

escape is lulled back
down with
lips

half-pucked
against a sag they
all but resist – thumb

more visible merely
than the lighter it
never quite gets

going – that
minimalist jigger
bug on your back so

slow–starting &
not the instant
waking

imagined to
show life must
find its jagged way

in & how life not
dying always
takes it

when milk enters

blood as floes that
blob lesser &
rounder into

reddened sea
so your far-shrilled
gull motions in circles to

whittle stillness then
drop to a pose
abruptly

local
quelled one
legged at an edge to

glance down-up this
main-street melt
whose vast

white Moores
loom & glob glide
purposefully south as

slugs diminish through
light salt-porous as if
waiting were due

till one suck
-sigh from waves
north-keeping rheums

the child-lucent span to
temperate foam
fizzes

to deep
water your fast
-shrinking ice-aspirin

of unsleep

this removal is

not so much
sleep through which
breath persists but more

what death
might be the known
return calming such moments

as these as
though each night upon
absenting ourselves we held for

certain we
must harbour back from
deep-swelled dream that a child

however taken
to quell the house were
not taken at all but just down

the mall
or heard on far-
sided silence laughing

someplace else

no matter

light marks
your form
as return

as though
opposing
cosmoses

leant &
pitched
against

to tent their
cancelling
forces till

from pure-
stacked an-
nihilation

merged im
-probable
residue

you : as
sole scale
left from

packed
seas or l-
one part

-icle from
far-flung
globe long

burst from
hard-round
pillow into

flocculating
flak – o you
radiate soft

& holy
gamma
that way

each probe
into dark
light is is

only dark
shown its
way & so

given back

with you water

burgeons this house
daylight a white
you

punctured –
one scud shadowed
on sand or those oval blues

dousing thirst near-black as you
on the inside water
yourself

with sleep
your own animal
banded in crib-light come to

its dream to lie with the tanned
predator shuddering news
to that spine to

your gosling
-down mullet & di-
stilled mulse-dribble as mead

wells each cornering eye to
make slumber this
slowed rite &

slumber that
vow my wakefulness
arouses the lower your breath

quick-sands itself & how word
-lost i stealth your hand
into mine

slight
as it is to take
you in health & in

my water want you as i do
for better or even
better

now resist

raise an arm to it
as if to be excused
the fall that kick

toward waters long
evaporated to thinly
eerie salts your rage

kin to bared sea-bed
detached & innard-
calm against living

light while rolled on
your side your spine
arches pained to let

skiffy vapours tic
under on last-puff
dread each enzyme

pulling as it must
until the sheet you
worry to cast-off

cloth shrouds you
whitely careless as
though you had fled

breath but were still
so warm no mother
tidal with pity nor

callused hand too
long below had
stowed courage

or could stir in
themselves that
slimmest billow

to trim you

blood content

until it presses
from within that
scarlet leaf blotching

once per cheek as if
skin were frosted
glass father

rarely sees
through flapped
into by dentate shapes

rain-driven from behind
the tree drops
to save

so
sudden wet
makes your martian hue

fiercer in its moment pinned
in pressure to honour
what by what

ever means
must push through
from wordless speech or

orderless form & each
child who registers
in blood

that opened
ledger from time
to time urges this all

-at-once unskinned
surface enflamed
by futures

begun for
now in a cry
that is not yet

sounded but
the ferociously
earthed splitting

seed

repetition not

merely rehearsed through
you but couched
in your way

secure as
that boulder a
well-worn jewel set

skew in its moor though
far less discernible
your rattled

copying
eager for itself
for all its vigour &

play with variety caught
in brown studies as
service to repro-

duction while
this two-eyed wink
in one barely born pulls

with it your automated
stitch of a smile &
that brick you

stretch for how
-ever small or un-
naturally coloured is

being put in its place
as flesh is lost
in praise

of bricks so
a father with shat-
-tered pate & no farther

than his gate seeks in worm
-cast hope & mountain
aspiration to

unrubble
how one might p-
luck your sweet-shapen head

stone clean & wet-shone
from black-lustred
peat without

breaking?

how you are   down

on one side shielding
noon arm across your face
as though sleep were blinding &

beyond you those zodiacal familiars
cartoon posed crabbily
strewn to lie on

odd rotations at odds
with their grins   your hillock
head bulges soft stones lengthens

its fescues unevenly reddish about ears
where more sun touched perhaps
each thumbnail a dusk

paring waxing its half
moon as every part you
cannot know & think i do

homes to your room to enjoin yet
still itself in ways i had all
but lost not least that

mother quiet
as a wall fallen so
cleanly awake in this

doze swooned by the hours
at last on her side now
sharp-sudden

as the first giant
undistanced through
scopes her rounded back

turned to yours light-barred
one arm-tip ringed
shadows

that too-soon face

now you stow

slow life breathward
a breath at a time
supine-strange

ship crewed
with self decked
in unruddered sinew

each arm-mast jointed
& cargoed bellows
that must force

quick
death out
as brine through

one insistent note shifting
its tack in the throat
to freshen

rhythmed
pitch as though all
those reefs now thinning

wakefulness to darker blues
might be known if
only keeled

singly & though
time is against you
still you fathom each

sound even while it slackens
in you in mounting
urgencies

this sailed-
through though
never over labour

i want to stay

for every way you
drop that chick-beak
wide to swallow torn-off

trust at times spat out though
being able to watch such
dust struck alive is

what time passes
for luck while slow fingers
pinch bread from dough testing

temperatures on elbow or tongue to
stop that slot-pink mouth
with timely hosts

this is not mine
to guarantee as you do
the unthought unseen behind

action soon to be lost to you or
sooner to me this gangue
we owe to crust &

stars they say though
bread so freed by you may
one day grow backward sting

while suns for all their pang & th-
rust cannot see for shine
nor know

now speech enters

you flight-eyed it seems
with landscaping
sounds we

murmur bluntly
tuning that rich mouth
informed somewhere between

beak & bloom our patter
persistent among those
twigging cells or

short-soft shouts
we pitch against that
cliffed face made distant

even as it shifts slightly back
into sun lean with late
afternoon it

feigns
never to have
known the torrents stacking

upstream these intermittent
trickles your headwater
stores in porous

bone you might
when the stresses decree
release jaws opening to what is

cleared by fluid being long-held
in your soon to green &
light-sprung

spring

no less than star

you spread light-solid four-limbed
compass-point diagonals via
brightened blood – our

journeys further gone in
intersected circles than any nucle-
us bred in blue-hot cores that unravelled

to talc puffed out into space as spores
that know how we loose
atomics must

eventually
bind to heat whatever that
finding founds: however sorry a speck

until infinitesimals mount – planets
constructing each arc through
us whose magmas lapse

unspoken as this
tiny hand willed against
gravity against another dark outheld

as wrinkled matter sufficient to wrap
your span – yet how that
cool pink palm

you brought to
mine barely the size of its
warmth distorts all space – all time

to eclipse

not so much that

churble snagged on each
draught spiralled up
to my study

more gull than bulbul on
its own thermal or
those features

discerned through
ceilings that out-glass
panes for certain wave-

lengths of attention or
our skew ventriloquism
whereby your few drop-

jaw gestures work me mute
while you perk control
up my back into

a hollowed-out
skull nor even hauled
up stairs that Velcro grip i

feel at your mother's ex-
posed neck : rather
one halved

hour in our
house you two
proudly left whose

closest-going cargo
to you is now
this dark

-clouding
window's cap-
sized cloud

that

when mortar fevers towards
winter – sweats on the inside

to shed summer down panes
icily one stream at a time in

downwardness disconcerted
pooling on sills serum so far

removed from veins it is lost
to what is pure yet lacking

specifics circulates much : so
you breathe here evenly &

calm as infant dawn sends light
chill through a home that stops

to view itself at frames whose
waters clear old against new

expended in order to touch
palms as children do across

glass where each finger tip to
tip senses pressure & whets

that flat-oval film but never
can quite cross as if autumn

without had struck on spring
within & with hazed silence

strained to buffet blameless
apertures just to enter this

father enflaming now in all
that

& a cloud passes

does for blue
what your leaving
brings to floor & glass

not one thing altered yet all
changed – the material
having made us

means to recall
what glides through
seemingly gone – such is

muscle unboned & gristle
relaxed by time a
cross which

feet shuffle
their same centurion
walk to carve imperceptibly

that hallowed curve worn
in stone so one may
suppose another

passed & an
-other here where
static walls bow out in

-finitesimally to keep you
somehow in mind-
less mind

until that snick
of the key – the hinge
turned almost from volition

that swing-squeals to your face
unweathered fusing
weathers

as if my look
were brick & room
fresh from the outside to

earth not least this blood
onto surface into
every pore

in wood &
fabric while neither
father nor hearth knows

for sure which
trembled
first

how heartwood is

the old hand
light-wrinkled

guides younger
fingers together

– push one plump
pulse through sand

then water ah feel
that pressure each

small yield in resi-
stance as pleasure

rises to flood what
is coldly scanned

in time : that stone
shifts with planting

worlds whose past
-ured loam stands

bent with shadow
to show itself now

thumbed & shoved
through death into

whatever might be
dared to life though

as the subtle earth
is palmed back over

neither quite known
nor knows which is

seed to whom

in slant light almost

you split that reed in its throat
so your solo half chant half sp-

uttered all but unshattered shards
till now mismatched back to that

clouded sheet where sun com-
poses the solemn window over

you : torso staved to differently
lit parts whose coda might have

been an utterance instead of this
near-found sound said precisely

over toned with closure though
never ajar to that   history

awaits you as rosin to stranded
facts or those borderless hordes

amassed against your palate's
softly upholstered double-door

which hinges onto instruments
half-raised charging the mur-

mur that civilizes before your
sudden orchestra slides into

tune hushed by a baton under
stood & standing to which

your next note might be
dark falling beyond all

noise or time finding
at last its key

tulip i

as a boy
pressed into
loam the hole

spoon-dug over
wide too
deep

a bulb
hairlessly gently
lobed firm with pressings

-out into world pure
white grazed
jaundice

where light
had caught but
plumped all over

raw-healthed keened
by aromas soil
makes

of itself
as if exuded
by vegetable flesh

coolly perspiring after
sun in pursuit of
its seeming

form yet
held by some
consistent chord in

ground so down you
go so shallow
& grave

let damp
life seep in
mould to you

as you ascend
make you
green